PIONEER VALLEY EDUCATIONAL PRESS, INC

HOW MANY
ANIMALS?

TRINA LAWRENCE

I can see three giraffes
and two puppies.
How many animals
can you see?

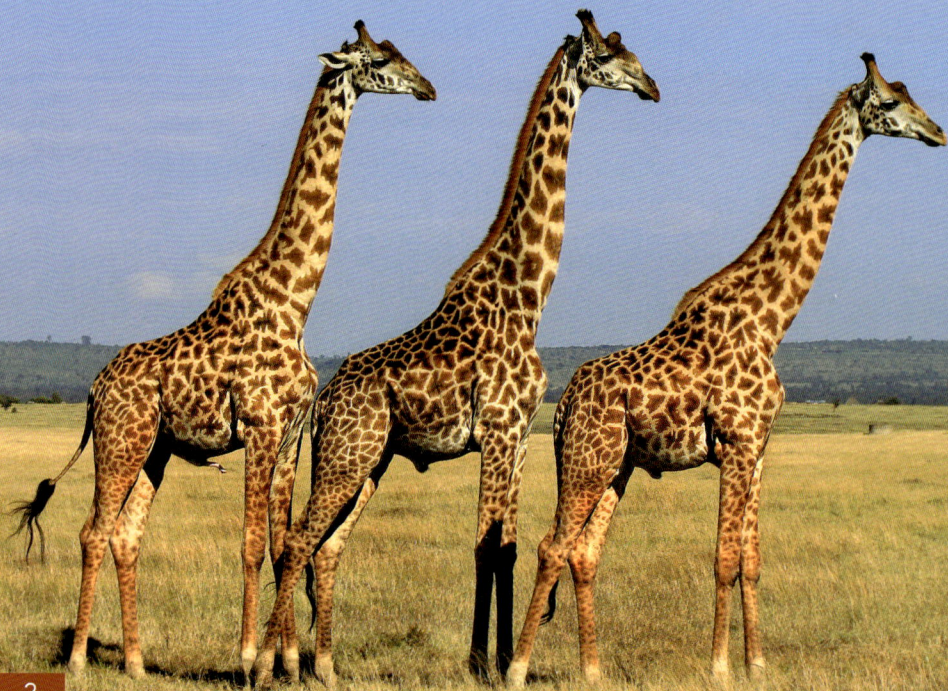

3 + 2 = 5

I can see one bear cub
and two horses.
How many animals
can you see?

1 + 2 = 3

I can see four lions
and two zebras.
How many animals
can you see?

$$4 + 2 = 6$$

I can see two foxes
and three lambs.
How many animals
can you see?

$$2 + 3 = 5$$

I can see three polar bears
and five penguins.
How many animals
can you see?

$$3 + 5 = 8$$

I can see five kittens
and four goats.
How many animals
can you see?

$$5 + 4 = 9$$

I can see five cows
and two meerkats.
How many animals
can you see?

$$5 + 2 = 7$$

1
one

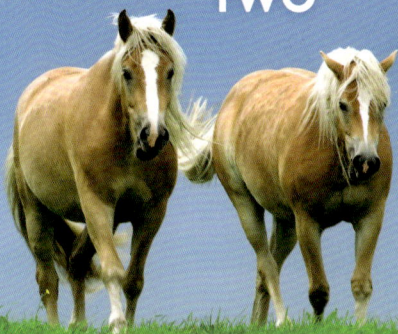

2
two

3
three

4
four

5
five